P9-CUK-107

CROSS-SECTIONS
THE HMMWV HUMVEE

by Steve Parker
illustrated by Alex Pang

Capstone press®

Mankato, Minnesota

Childrens Department
Menasha's Public Library
440 1st Street
Menasha, WI 54952

Edge Books are published by Capstone Press, a Coughlan Publishing Company,
151 Good Counsel Drive, P.O. Box 669, Mankato, Minnesota 56002.
www.capstonepress.com

Copyright © 2008 by David West Children's Books.
All rights reserved.
No part of this publication may be reproduced in whole or in part, or stored in a retrieval
system, or transmitted in any form or by any means, electronic, mechanical,
photocopying, recording, or otherwise, without written permission of the publisher.
For information regarding permission, write to Capstone Press,
151 Good Counsel Drive, P.O. Box 669, Dept. R, Mankato, Minnesota 56002.
Printed in the United States of America

Library of Congress Cataloging-in-Publication Data
Parker, Steve.
    The HMMWV Humvee/by Steve Parker; illustrated by Alex Pang.
    p. cm.—(Edge books. Cross-sections)
    Summary: "An in-depth look at the HMMWV Humvee, with detailed
cross-section diagrams, action photos, and fascinating facts"—Provided by publisher.
    Includes bibliographical references and index.
    ISBN-13: 978-1-4296-0093-4 (hardcover)
    ISBN-10: 1-4296-0093-4 (hardcover)
    1. Hummer trucks—Juvenile literature. I. Title.
UG618.P37 2008
623.7'4722—dc22   2007005938

Designed and produced by

David West ♀♂ Children's Books
7 Princeton Court
55 Felsham Road
Putney
London SW15 1AZ

Designer: Rob Shone
Editor: Gail Bushnell

Photo Credits
U.S. Navy, 1, 7t, 24, 28–29, 29; U.S. Army, 4–5, 16, 17, 18, 20–21, 22, 25tl, 25tr;
Library of Congress, 6; AM General, 7b; U.S. Air Force, 10, 11, 14, 19; U.S. Marine
Corps, 12, 23, 25b, 28

Humvee is a registered trademark of AM General.

1 2 3 4 5 6 12 11 10 09 08 07

TABLE OF CONTENTS

HMMWV 4

A Humvee History 6

Cross-Section. 8

The Engine 10

The Chassis 12

The Body 14

Interior 16

Weapons 18

TOW Missile. 20

Avenger. 22

Other Variants. 24

The Mission 26

The Future 28

Glossary 30

Read More. 31

Internet Sites 31

Index 32

HMMWV

HMMWV means High Mobility Multi-purpose Wheeled Vehicle. This is a long name so it is shortened to "Hmm-V" or "Humvee" to make it easier to say.

The Humvee is a lightweight, all-terrain vehicle. It has a powerful diesel engine and four-wheel drive. It is used mainly by the military forces.

Humvees are so useful because they can be adapted with different fittings and equipment for many roles. These include scouting around the battlefield and carrying troops, arms, ammunition, and supplies. Humvees can also carry big guns and missiles. They are used to pull trailers and are sometimes fitted out as ambulances.

There is a big gap between the Humvee's wide body and the ground, called ground clearance. This allows it to travel over very bumpy ground without scraping or other damage.

A HUMVEE HISTORY

The Humvee is the latest in a long series of small, mobile, adaptable military vehicles.

THE JEEP STORY

One of the best-known vehicles in the world is the army jeep. It was originally called a General Purpose (GP) Vehicle. This name was later changed to jeep.

The jeep was designed and built in less than 49 days. It was built during World War II (1939–1945), when the U.S. government urgently needed a small, go-anywhere vehicle.

Early military vehicles were little more than ordinary cars covered with sheets of armor plating for protection.

Willys-Overland Motors and the Ford Motor Company built more than 700,000 jeeps in the United States during World War II.

The jeep was a huge success, but by the 1970s, it was getting old. So the U.S. government asked American car companies for a bigger, tougher replacement—the Humvee.

INTO PRODUCTION

Early Humvees were built in the early 1980s by the AM General Company. In 1983, they were tested and accepted by the U.S. government. The first contract was for 55,000 Humvees at a cost of $1.2 billion. More big orders followed in 1989 and 1994. After 1995, stronger, more powerful versions were made, such as the A2 and ECV (Expanded Capacity Vehicle) Humvees.

Humvees are built in South Bend, Indiana, and shipped for military duty all over the world.

One of the Humvee's most famous features is its seven-slot front grill. It lets in air to cool the huge diesel engine.

CROSS-SECTION

The Humvee is designed to come apart easily so that its main parts can be altered for different roles. This is one reason why it's such a good multipurpose vehicle.

The many versions of the Humvee look different on the outside. They can be different inside, too. Some have bigger, more powerful engines. Others have a stronger chassis (framework) and suspension for carrying heavier loads or more armor. Some Humvees have a bigger fuel tank to travel farther between refills.

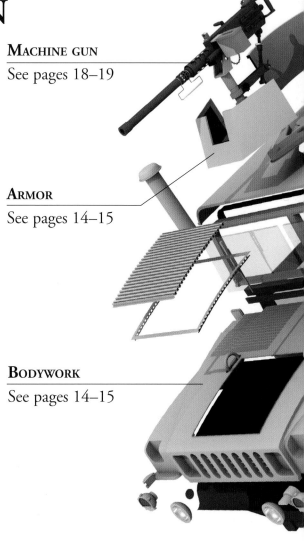

MACHINE GUN
See pages 18–19

ARMOR
See pages 14–15

BODYWORK
See pages 14–15

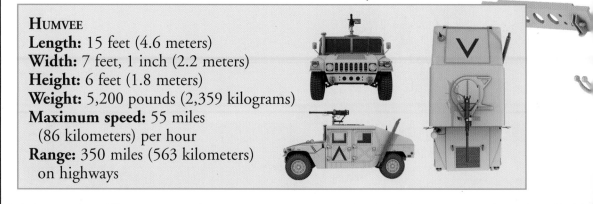

HUMVEE
Length: 15 feet (4.6 meters)
Width: 7 feet, 1 inch (2.2 meters)
Height: 6 feet (1.8 meters)
Weight: 5,200 pounds (2,359 kilograms)
Maximum speed: 55 miles
  (86 kilometers) per hour
Range: 350 miles (563 kilometers)
  on highways

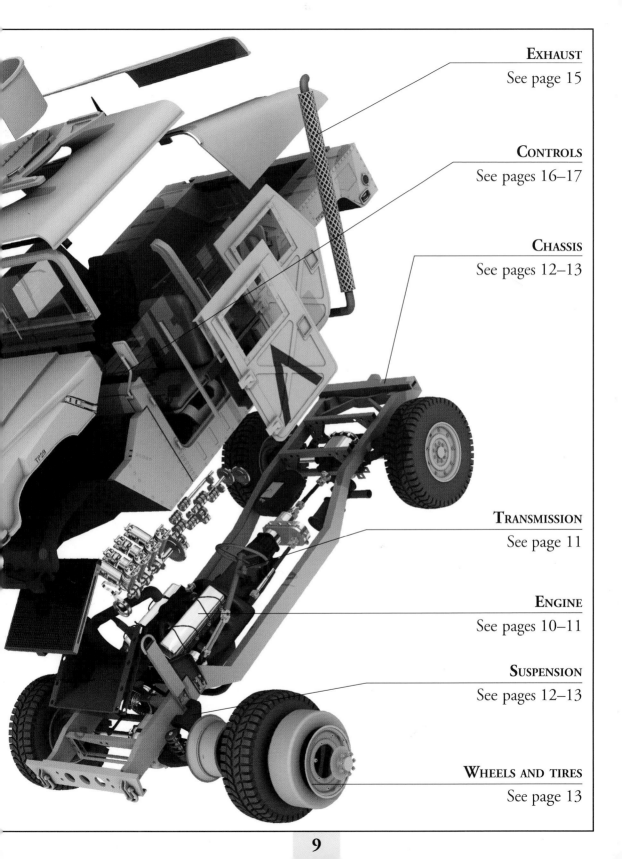

EXHAUST

See page 15

CONTROLS

See pages 16–17

CHASSIS

See pages 12–13

TRANSMISSION

See page 11

ENGINE

See pages 10–11

SUSPENSION

See pages 12–13

WHEELS AND TIRES

See page 13

THE ENGINE

The Humvee's 6.2-liter engine was upgraded in 1995 to a 6.5-liter engine. This powerful engine gives the Humvee a top speed of more than 70 miles (113 kilometers) per hour.

The Humvee engine is strong, rugged, and reliable. It can be taken apart quickly for servicing and repair, using few specialized tools. This is important when Humvees are in action in remote areas, where they are far from garages.

CYLINDERS

There are eight cylinders in two rows of four. The cylinders are not upright, but at an angle to each other, like the sides of the letter "V." This design gives the name V8.

GLOW PLUGS

When starting the engine in cold weather, electricity passes through the glow plugs. It makes them very hot. This helps the fuel-air mixture catch fire and explode.

As the 650-pound (295-kilogram) engine is lifted out in the workshop, all of its parts can be reached.

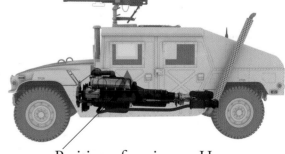

Position of engine on Humvee

TRANSMISSION

The original Humvees had an automatic gearbox (no gear shift) with three forward speeds and one reverse. Newer transmissions have four forward speeds and one reverse.

The engine, electrical wires, air intakes, and exhaust are all high up inside the watertight Humvee. It keeps running in water 5 feet (1.5 meters) deep.

FOUR-WHEEL DRIVE LINKAGE

Some off-road vehicles have a choice of two- or four-wheel drive. The Humvee is four-wheel drive all the time, meaning that the engine powers all four road wheels. This means better grip and less wheelspin on slippery mud and ice.

ENGINE SPECIFICATIONS
The latest Humvees have an AM General Optimizer 6.5-liter V8 diesel engine with fuel injection. It produces 190 horsepower (hp).

THE CHASSIS

The chassis is the main frame of a vehicle. All the other parts are fitted onto it.

The chassis is the same basic size and shape in all Humvees. It looks like a ladder of steel girders or rails all welded together. The mid-frame is the largest, with shorter front and rear frames. Some later versions of the Humvee have a stronger chassis to carry heavier loads.

The "droppable" Humvee can be carried by a helicopter sling. It can also be released from a cargo plane to drift down by parachute.

SUSPENSION
Each wheel has a double wishbone independent suspension with coil springs. Hydraulic dampers, or shock absorbers, soak up the jolts and shakes.

WHEEL AND TIRE

The extra-tough tires are 37 inches (94 centimeters) high and 12.5 inches (31.8 centimeters) wide. They have a low-profile "run-flat" design, meaning they can go a short way even if punctured.

REAR FRAME RAIL

The rear frame supports the rear suspension. It also has a towing hitch for pulling trailers.

POWER STEERING

Energy from the engine assists the steering. The steering wheel is movable with just one finger.

BRAKES

All four wheels have power-assisted disk brakes for maximum stopping power.

CTIS

The Central Tire Inflation System (CTIS) lets the crew members change the air pressure in the tires while on the move. They can lower the pressure for softer tires on bumpy ground or increase it for highways.

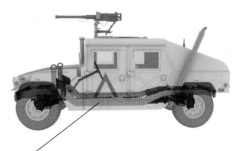

Position of chassis on Humvee

THE BODY

The Humvee's main bodywork is lightweight aluminum. This can be strengthened with extra sheets and plates for the battlefield.

The aluminum panels are joined by rivets and also bonded, or glued, using the latest high-technology adhesives. Aluminum is not only light and strong, but it also does not rust or corrode.

The Humvee's bodywork is not totally stiff or rigid. This allows it to twist and flex slightly, rather than crack or split as the vehicle roars across bumpy ground.

AIR INTAKE
Air for the engine enters through a high intake, above the dusty road and water spray.

Body panels that are damaged, such as by gunfire, can be replaced quickly. Humvees that are going into battle have extra armor added. They are called "up-armored" Humvees.

CUPOLA

The cupola, a small structure that can turn around, is ring-mounted in the roof. It is used by observers and gunners.

EXHAUST

The angled exhaust directs fumes upward and sideways, away from following vehicles.

BULLET-PROOF GLASS

The windscreen is toughened for protection against flying rocks and even bullets. It cracks or "crazes" rather than shattering into pieces.

SIDE ARMOR

Armor strips along the sides and below the doors guard against land mines and other low blasts.

SKID/ARMOR PLATES

Extra metal sheets on the underside protect against exploding land mines.

INTERIOR

Inside, the Humvee is not especially comfortable. It has to be basic so that it is light and so it has space for the crew members, their equipment, and the weapons.

It can get very hot inside a Humvee. To keep cool, crew members can wear vests that are connected to a small air conditioning unit.

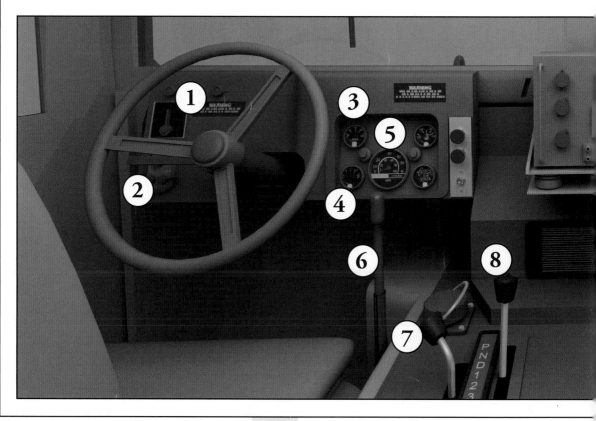

Humvees usually have two or four seats, depending on how many crew members are needed for the job. A radio and tracking screen are used by the crew to talk to other crews and identify target positions.

The Blue Force Tracking system displays vehicle locations on a screen map. It sends voice or text messages in military code via satellite to the command center.

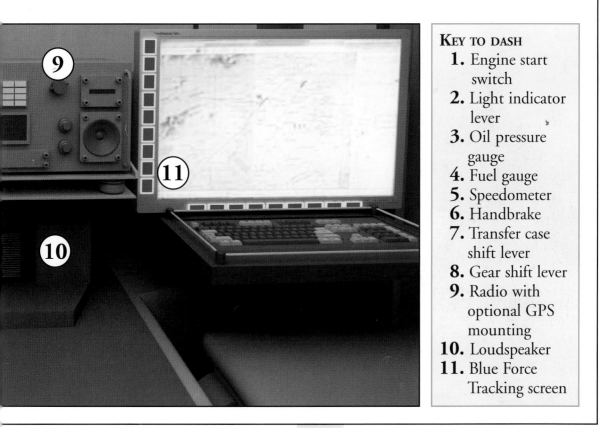

KEY TO DASH
1. Engine start switch
2. Light indicator lever
3. Oil pressure gauge
4. Fuel gauge
5. Speedometer
6. Handbrake
7. Transfer case shift lever
8. Gear shift lever
9. Radio with optional GPS mounting
10. Loudspeaker
11. Blue Force Tracking screen

WEAPONS

The gunner keeps close watch as the soldiers search for hidden weapons.

One of the Humvee's common weapons is a heavy machine gun, such as the M2 Browning Machine Gun (BMG), mounted in the cupola.

M2 .50 CALIBER HEAVY MACHINE GUN
The M2 is a recoil-operated machine gun. The recoil, or kickback, from each bullet creates energy. This energy is used to remove the spent round and insert the next one.

BREECH

The rounds are on a long belt that feeds through the breech. The breech is the chamber from which the bullets are fired.

AMMUNITION
The "fifty-cal" bullets weigh 1.6 ounces (45 grams) each. They travel up to 2,000 miles (3,219 kilometers) per hour.

The Humvee can also carry the Mk 19 grenade launcher. It fires up to 60 grenades in a minute and has a range of more than 1 mile (1.6 kilometers).

Barrel

A .50 caliber gun has a barrel with a hole inside for the bullet that is 0.50 inches (1.3 centimeters) wide.

The machine gun swings around in a circle as the gunner stands in the area normally occupied by the two rear passengers.

A typical heavy machine gun could fire more than 500 times per minute, but this would wear it out quickly. Guns like the M2 are limited to 40 bullets or less per minute. The M2's maximum range is 4 miles (6.4 kilometers).

TOW MISSILE

TOW stands for Tube-launched, Optically tracked, Wire command-link. The Humvee becomes a mobile missile launcher when equipped with the deadly TOW missile.

The TOW missile is launched by a tube that looks like a short, wide gun barrel. As the missile leaves, it pulls behind two thin wires that connect back to the launcher.

The TOW missile is mounted on the cupola. Up to three TOWs can be launched in 90 seconds.

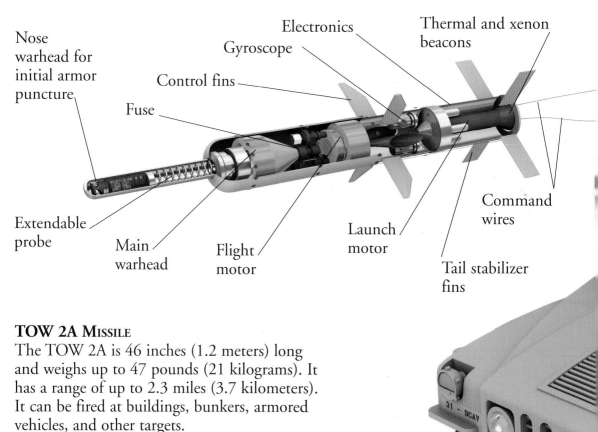

Nose warhead for initial armor puncture

Control fins

Fuse

Gyroscope

Electronics

Thermal and xenon beacons

Extendable probe

Main warhead

Flight motor

Launch motor

Command wires

Tail stabilizer fins

TOW 2A Missile
The TOW 2A is 46 inches (1.2 meters) long and weighs up to 47 pounds (21 kilograms). It has a range of up to 2.3 miles (3.7 kilometers). It can be fired at buildings, bunkers, armored vehicles, and other targets.

As the missile flies, the operator aims it at the target optically (by sight). The thin wires carry command signals to the missile to adjust its course.

LAUNCH SYSTEM

Each TOW missile comes ready to fire with its own disposable fiberglass tube, wires, and other parts.

NIGHT SIGHT

The thermal (heat-sensing) night sight can identify hazards such as enemy fire.

T/X SENSORS

T/X sensors track the missile's xenon and thermal infrared beacons that give the missile's position.

AVENGER

The Avenger is a missile system of eight Stinger heat-seeking missiles. It is mounted onto a Humvee that has been specially strengthened.

The machine gun can protect the Avenger from low-flying enemy aircraft.

CANOPY

The protective canopy screen gives the missile operator a clear forward view.

RANGEFINDER

An eye-safe, infrared laser rangefinder measures distances. It is accurate even at night. The missile and target are tracked on video.

MISSILE POD

Each of the two pods contains four missiles. These are usually Stingers, but other pod designs are available for different missiles, such as the Javelin.

MACHINE GUN

A .50 caliber machine gun, as shown earlier, is included mainly for self-defense.

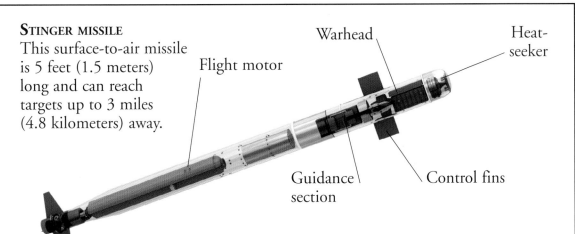

STINGER MISSILE
This surface-to-air missile is 5 feet (1.5 meters) long and can reach targets up to 3 miles (4.8 kilometers) away.

Warhead

Heat-seeker

Flight motor

Guidance section

Control fins

Tailfin

The Avenger operator sits between the two launch pods. A blast screen protects him from the blast of the missiles.

Avengers are mainly for air defense—shooting down enemy missiles or warplanes. The Avenger missiles can be fired while the vehicle is on the move. The strengthened Humvees used to carry Avengers are code-numbered M998, M1097, and M1123.

OTHER VARIANTS

The Humvee's multipurpose roles include mobile radio control center, supplies carrier, and even ambulance.

The Humvee has more than 40 parts which can be easily changed for different tasks, providing more than 15 versions. These are all fitted onto the basic chassis and engine. The M1097 series can carry extra-heavy loads of almost 2 tons (1.8 metric tons).

A Humvee equipped with radio and microwave antennas and a revolving radar can act as a mobile command center.

M1097 CONTACT MAINTENANCE TRUCK
The M1097 carries a large container of supplies, including tools, parts, and spare tires. It is used to help with on-the-spot repair of almost any piece of equipment, even an airplane.

The M1037 transports the S250 Shelter, a container for electronic and communications equipment.

Some Humvees are used as troop transports or personnel carriers.

M997A1 MAXI-AMBULANCE
The M997 is known as the "maxi-ambulance." It can carry four stretchers or up to eight "walking wounded." Kevlar armor provides good protection as it transports.

There are several Humvee ambulance versions. The M996 and M997 are hardtops. The smaller M1035 has a soft top, making it lighter and faster.

This tracked Humvee is being tested near Bridgeport, California, for use in icy and snowy regions.

THE MISSION

Every day, thousands of Humvees see action across the world. Some are on training missions, while others are being used in real conflicts.

Humvees are so adaptable that the crews can carry out entire missions by themselves. They use variants such as scout vehicles, troop carriers, supply transports, and Avenger missile launchers. A typical mission might involve avoiding an ambush while escorting a convoy of arms and ammunition to the front line.

2. An Avenger Humvee detects possible enemies in the distance, using its thermal (heat) imaging sensors.

1. A convoy of large supply trucks drives through the desert, escorted and guarded by Humvees.

3. Scout Humvees move in fast to investigate.

4. The Humvees discover an enemy force waiting in a small village, ready to ambush the convoy.

5. Troop-carrying Humvees arrive. The soldiers drive away the enemy and prevent the ambush.

THE FUTURE

By 2007, almost 200,000 Humvees had been built for the United States and 50 of its friendly countries. How long can its design last?

The Humvee dates back more than 20 years and has been continually upgraded and improved. Today's engines produce almost twice as much power as the early versions. But the Humvee was never designed to be a combat vehicle. Even up-armored Humvees can be damaged or destroyed by land mines and rocket-propelled grenades.

Could the Humvee's replacement look like this? The Ultra AP armored patrol car uses race car technology to keep its crew safe.

Like the Humvee, the Cougar can transport troops. It is heavily armored to protect the people inside from roadside bombs. It cannot do as many different jobs as the Humvee though.

The U.S. Armed Forces want to replace the Humvee with vehicles that can survive the modern battlefield. But the Humvee will not disappear just yet. Humvees will still be needed to transport troops and cargo, act as ambulances, and perform many other tasks while newer combat vehicles do the dangerous jobs.

The Humvee is an easy vehicle to drive, repair, and maintain. Military mechanics are well trained in servicing the Humvee and spare parts are easy to get. It may take three or four new vehicle designs to replace the Humvee.

The Shadow Reconnaissance Surveillance Targeting Vehicle (RST-V) may also take on some of the Humvee's work. It is called a hybrid because it has a diesel engine and electric motors. If it uses just its electric motors, it is very quiet and stealthy.

GLOSSARY

chassis (CHASS-ee)—the main framework of a vehicle to which the other parts are fixed

cupola (KYOO-puh-luh)—the small turret set onto the roof in many kinds of Humvees

four-wheel drive (FOR-WEEL DRIVE)—a system that transfers engine power to all four wheels of a vehicle for better grip

horsepower (HORSS-pou-ur)—the measurement of an engine's power, abbreviated as hp

mission (MIH-shuhn)—a task given to a person or group

suspension (suss-PEN-shun)—the tilting arms, springs, dampers, and other parts that smooth out road bumps so a vehicle's ride is more comfortable

stealth (STELTH)—the ability to move without being detected

variant (VARE-ee-uhnt)—a modified, adapted, or changed version compared to the main or standard version

READ MORE

Baker, David. *M1097 Humvee.* Fighting Forces on Land. Vero Beach, Fla.: Rourke, 2007.

Healy, Nick. *High Mobility Vehicles: The Humvees.* War Machines. Mankato, Minn.: Capstone Press, 2005.

Teitelbaum, Michael. *Humvees: High Mobility in the Field.* Mighty Military Machines. Berkeley Heights, N.J.: Enslow, 2006.

INTERNET SITES

FactHound offers a safe, fun way to find Internet sites related to this book. All of the sites on FactHound have been researched by our staff.

Here's how:
1. Visit *www.facthound.com*
2. Choose your grade level.
3. Type in this book ID **1429600934** for age-appropriate sites. You may also browse subjects by clicking on letters, or by clicking on pictures and words.
4. Click on the **Fetch It** button.

FactHound will fetch the best sites for you!

INDEX

ambulances, 4, 24, 25, 29

ammunition, 4, 18, 26

armor, 6, 8, 14, 15, 20, 25, 28

Avenger, 22–23, 26

Blue Force Tracking system, 17

bodywork, 8, 14–15

brakes, 13

chassis, 8, 12–13, 24

Central Tire Inflation System (CTIS), 13

cupola, 15, 18, 20

ECV Humvees, 7

engine, 4, 7, 8, 10–11, 13, 14, 24, 28, 29

exhaust, 11, 15

four-wheel drive, 4, 11

gearbox, 11

glow plugs, 10

ground clearance, 5

jeeps, 6

M1097 Contact Maintenance Truck, 24

machine gun, 18–19, 22

night sight, 21

radio, 17, 24

rangefinder, 22

speed, 8, 10

steering, 13

Stinger missiles, 22–23

suspension, 8, 12, 13

tires, 13, 24

TOW missile, 20–21

up-armored Humvees, 14, 28

wheels, 11, 12, 13

World War II, 6